TOPZ 10 HEROES OF THE BIBLE...

If you like stories then you're going to just LOVE reading about Josie and Sarah's Topz 10 Bible heroes!

The Bible is absolutely bursting full with tales of men and women who left their 'ordinary' selves far behind, and became heroes for God.

Through God's power:

- **Timid people can be bold**

- **Scared people can be brave**

- **Confused people can find the answers to their problems**

- **Hurt people can learn to forgive**

- **Doubtful people can grow their faith**

- **Worried people can start to trust**

- **Unlikely people can become God's super-workers!**

You're about to discover 10 people from the Bible who had a sense of adventure and enough faith to live full-on for God – wherever that took them, and whatever it led them to do! What mattered was putting God first, living the way He wanted them to live, and doing what He asked them to do.

Following God like that isn't easy. It means trusting Him to help you in everything – and believing that He will never stop loving you.

Let the 10 heroes in this book fill you up with excitement and show you that life with God is **THE ABSOLUTE FANDABULOUS BEST!**

Fill in and decorate the next page, then – happy reading!

My name is

_____

**and I want to learn
how to be a**

HERO!

RUTH
The faithful friend
Read all about her in the book of *RUTH*

Do you have a best friend? Someone you like to hang around with as much as possible? Someone you can chat to about anything – good and bad things, happy and sad things, weird and wacky things?

Do you have a best friend like that?

> Psst! I have! It's Josie. I think it'll always be Josie. But don't tell her, or she might get big-headed!

But did you know that *being* a best friend is just as important as *having* a best friend?

How would you describe a really good friend? Think of as many different words as you can (for example, kind, patient), and write them down here.

_____

_____

_____

The book of Ruth in the Old Testament of the Bible tells the story of a woman who was an amazing friend.

Her name was Ruth
– believe it or not!

THE STORY BEGINS WITH A WOMAN CALLED NAOMI.
She and her family (her husband and their two sons) had to move away from their home in Bethlehem. There was very little food there, so they went to live in a place called Moab, where there was plenty to eat.

But Naomi's new life didn't work out at all like she hoped. First her husband died, and then, a few years later, she lost both her sons too.

That's the sad part of the story, but it gets a lot happier.

Naomi's sons had got married while they lived in Moab. Their wives' names were Orpah and – yes, you guessed it – Ruth. Things were better in Bethlehem now and there was enough food again. So Naomi decided to go back there – back to her real home.

But did she ask Ruth and Orpah to go with her?

8

No – which was crazy! Without them, Naomi would have to make the journey all the way back to Bethlehem on her own. And, once she got there, she'd have to live on her own too. She'd lost all her family in Moab.

But, you see, Naomi was trying to be kind. Just as Bethlehem was her real home, Moab was Ruth and Orpah's real home. Naomi thought they would have a better life if they stayed there. It's where they belonged, with their own families. Naomi hoped they would get married again.

In the end, Orpah agreed. She said goodbye to Naomi and stayed in Moab. But Ruth – well – crack the code and write out the words to discover what she said.

'⏁⏁▷⊽⊲⊽⊲⊽⊲ ⊞⊽□ ⊙⊽, □ ⏁⏁□⊟⊟ ⊙⊽; ⏁⏁▷⊽⊲⊽⊲⊽⊲ ⊞⊽□ ⊟□⊲⊽, □ ⏁⏁□⊟⊟ ⊟□⊲⊽. ⊞⊽□⊲ ▷⊽⊽▷⊟⊽ ⏁⏁□⊟⊟ ⊠⊽ ⋀⊞ ▷⊽⊽▷⊟⊽, ⋀⊠▷ ⊞⊽□⊲ ⊙⊽▷ ⏁⏁□⊟⊟ ⊠⊽ ⋀⊞ ⊙⊽▷.'

A	B	C	D	E	F	G	H	I	J	K	L	M
N	O	P	Q	R	S	T	U	V	W	X	Y	Z

_____

_____

_____

_____

Answer in Ruth 1 v 16.

9

So Naomi and Ruth left Moab together – and Ruth was an incredibly good friend to her. Just look at what she did:

- **Ruth left her home and her family far behind so that Naomi didn't have to be alone.**
- **She did whatever she could to help Naomi.**
- **She didn't ask for anything in return.**

Very sad things had happened in Naomi's life. Ruth could see that what she really needed was someone to comfort her and be her friend. People need to be comforted for all sorts of reasons. Here are a few from some of the Gang.

When Gran wasn't well and Mum went to stay with her, Sarah was really upset and needed lots of comfort. She was worried about Gran and she didn't like Mum not being at home.

One of my friends at school had a pet cat. When it died, he was so upset he wouldn't eat his lunch.

I fell out with Benny over something silly. We made up, but before we did, it was horrible.

If one of your friends or someone in your family was unhappy, how could you comfort them? Write down some ideas here.

_____

_____

_____

Do you know someone who needs a good friend right now? Ask God to show you the best way to help them.

When Naomi and Ruth arrived in Bethlehem, they had nothing. But it was harvest time, so Ruth went to work in the fields. Poor people were allowed to walk behind the harvest workers and pick up the grain they dropped.

A man called Boaz owned the field where Ruth was working. As it happened, Boaz was related to Naomi's husband who'd died.

When Boaz found out what a good friend Ruth was being to Naomi, he decided to help her. He told her to work only in his field where she would be safe. He said she could help herself to water from the workers' jars. He even told his workers to drop extra grain in the field so that there was more for Ruth to collect and share with Naomi.

Now, Naomi loved God. But when all the bad things happened to her, she must have felt as if He didn't care about her anymore. Back in Bethlehem, she even asked people to stop calling her 'Naomi' – which means 'pleasant' – and call her 'Marah' instead. 'Marah' means 'bitter'.

But Naomi was wrong! **GOD LOVED HER AND WAS RIGHT BESIDE HER EVERY SINGLE MOMENT.** No matter how difficult and sad things were, He was working away to turn it all into something wonderful!

And guess who was going to be a hero in God's plan? Easy-peasy, isn't it? Trace over these letters to find out!

Which of the following sentences are true and which are false? Mark the true ones with a tick and the false ones with a cross.

1. God wanted Naomi to be unhappy. ☐

2. God made sure Naomi wasn't on her own. ☐

3. Ruth didn't care that Naomi was sad and lonely. ☐

4. God knew exactly what Naomi needed. ☐

5. Ruth and Naomi went hungry because God didn't help them. ☐

6. God looked after Naomi by making sure she had a good friend. ☐

7. Ruth was exactly the sort of friend God wanted her to be. ☐

8. Ruth was God's gift to Naomi. ☐

Answers on page 109.

The more Ruth learned about God, the more like Him she became – and the more God could use her to do good things!

Not only did God use Ruth to look after Naomi and make sure she wasn't left all alone – He found someone to do exactly the same thing for Ruth. Ruth and Boaz ended up getting married, and having a baby boy, called Obed.

Naomi must have been so proud and so happy! Now she had a new family to belong to: a family to look after her – and one she could look after.

But what Naomi didn't know was just how special this new family was…

Obed became the grandfather of King David. David was an ancestor of Joseph, who married Mary – who gave birth to Jesus!

Wow! When God makes a plan, He REALLY makes a plan! After all the sad things that had happened, God made Naomi and Ruth a part of Jesus' family line!

Flick back to page 7 and read through your list of words to describe a really good friend. Do you think most (or maybe all) of them would describe Ruth?

Even though Ruth had lost so much, she still gave up everything to help someone else lonely and in trouble. And God rewarded her for what she had done, and for learning to trust Him too.

And the people of Bethlehem noticed! Read what they said to Naomi in the read-around.

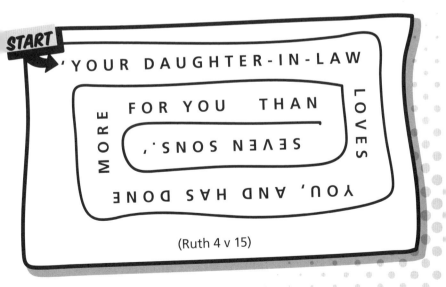

START

'YOUR DAUGHTER-IN-LAW LOVES YOU, AND HAS DONE MORE FOR YOU THAN SEVEN SONS.'

(Ruth 4 v 15)

SO – can you see why we chose **RUTH** to be **NUMBER 1** of our Topz 10 Bible heroes?

Ruth was… (Unscramble the letters.)

1. lihtfFua _____

2. ngvLoi _____

3. itPnate _____

4. nKid _____

5. gwHaonrkidr _____

6. shUnlesif _____

Answers on page 109.

Now that's how to be a real hero!

Here's a prayer for you to say to God...

Thank You, God, for Ruth – a hero for Naomi and a hero for You. Her story teaches me so much about being kind and faithful, and putting other people first. Please help me to remember all that she did for Naomi, and to try to be like her with my family and my friends. Thank You, too, that even when things are going badly, You will never leave me alone. You are my faithful friend. Amen.

2 NAAMAN'S SERVANT
Girl with a message
Read all about her in *2 KINGS 5*

Heroes come in all shapes and sizes. God's heroes tend to be unexpected – unexpected by other people and totally unexpected by the heroes themselves! But you still might be a bit surprised by the next girl to feature in our Topz 10.

Number 2 isn't a grown-up, and she isn't even given a name. In the story you're about to read, she only really has a tiny part to play. *BUT THAT TINY PART MADE A HUGE DIFFERENCE.*

This girl hero was an Israelite – one of God's special people – but she didn't live in Israel anymore. She had been captured by the king of Syria's army and taken to work as a slave. And she wasn't alone. Lots of God's people were now slaves in Syria.

But this particular girl was chosen to work in a very special job. She would be a servant for the wife of the Syrian army's commander. Very important! But not so much because of the household she worked in – because of what she was able to do for God there.

The Syrian army's commander was called Naaman. He was brilliant at his job. Everyone respected him, and even the king of Syria thought he was brilliant. So everything was groovy-doovy!

Except that it wasn't.

Naaman had an illness – a skin disease called leprosy. It was horrible. Nasty sores appeared on his skin, getting worse and worse. And, worst of all, there was no cure. In spite of Naaman's high position and being so well thought of by the king, no one could help him.

Everyone who knew Naaman was very sad to see him so ill. They were probably a bit nervous to get close to him too. Leprosy was very contagious, which means you could easily catch it. And how sad must Naaman's wife have felt. She and Naaman should have been happy together and had a good life. But Naaman's sickness would have spoilt it.

I hate being ill. I've been told I whinge a lot when I'm ill.

He really does.

Naaman didn't know God, so he didn't ask God to help him. But his wife's servant girl from Israel knew God very well. And she was about to introduce him…

Do you know what a 'prophet' is? A prophet is someone chosen by God to speak to people for Him. In Old Testament times, if God had something really important to say, he asked a prophet to deliver His message.

There are lots of prophets in the Bible. Some of them wrote books that you can find in the Old Testament.

Here's a list of a few of God's prophets. See if you can find them in the word search. You'll have to look carefully because some of the spellings are quite hard!

ELISHA
ELIJAH
ISAIAH
SAMUEL
JOEL
MOSES
JEREMIAH
AMOS
EZEKIEL
HAGGAI
JONAH
NATHAN

R	J	O	N	A	H	C	D	E	E	Z	I
R	A	E	B	S	M	Y	C	F	G	A	Y
Y	O	Z	R	T	I	O	G	E	D	R	L
T	E	E	N	E	B	M	S	L	X	E	B
R	T	K	N	H	M	W	H	I	O	L	X
M	E	I	O	P	R	I	T	J	U	I	V
E	R	E	R	N	I	S	A	A	T	S	W
O	A	L	P	A	O	A	J	H	R	H	M
B	G	D	G	T	O	I	K	S	Q	A	O
S	R	G	J	H	K	A	L	H	Q	P	S
C	A	Y	O	A	S	H	T	N	O	O	E
H	M	U	Y	N	G	L	E	U	M	A	S

Answer on page 109.

The servant girl was sad to see Naaman so sick. She was sad for his unhappy wife too, and for all the worrying that went on.

But even though no one could come up with a cure, the girl knew that there was a great big God who could make Naaman better, just like that – if only Naaman would turn to Him.

She also knew that all Naaman needed to do to get God's help was go and see one of God's prophets.

Colour in the dotted shapes to discover which prophet it was.

But the girl was an Israelite, and a slave. Would Naaman and his wife believe her? And, more to the point, would she be brave enough to say anything? Would she even really want to?

Try to imagine yourself in the servant girl's shoes, just for a minute…

- **An army has swept into your country.**
- **You've been captured and taken away from your home and your family.**
- **You've been forced to work as a slave in a new country.**
- **Your life has been turned upside down.**
- **You have no idea if you'll ever see your own home again.**

Now, still 'in her shoes', write down how you think you'd feel about your new master/mistress.

_____

_____

_____

Most of us would have been pretty furious if we'd found ourselves in this girl's position. But whether the servant girl was mad or not; whether she felt Naaman deserved God's help or not; whether she was scared even to mention God to people who didn't believe in Him or not – she showed her true hero self.

The servant girl put God, and Naaman's need, before her own feelings. And she told Naaman's wife where her husband could go to get help.

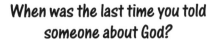

When was the last time you told someone about God?

The servant girl found herself somewhere special – in a place where she could tell someone about her Father God. And she took the opportunity. If we ask Him to, God will give *us* opportunities to tell other people about Him too!

God wants everyone – the whole world – to hear about Him. He wants us all to know that, through believing in His Son, Jesus, we can one day live with Him forever.

But God needs US to get out there and let people know who He is. Just like the servant girl did.

Who first told you about God?

_____

If you've told someone about God, how did you feel about talking to them?

_____

Remember that God never asks us to do anything by ourselves. If He puts you with someone who needs to hear about Him, **HE WILL BE WITH YOU TO HELP YOU FIND THE RIGHT WORDS.**

Talking to people about God is important. *Showing* God to people is important too.

Naaman's story doesn't tell us much about the servant girl. But it seems very clear that she was obedient and did her best for Naaman and his wife.

Even though she'd been taken away from her home, the girl behaved the way she knew God would want her to behave.

Have a look through this list. Put a tick beside the things that show God to others, and a cross beside the things that don't.

1. Being the friend someone really needs ☐

2. Being polite to teachers at school ☐

3. Not bothering to give something back that you've borrowed ☐

4. Standing up for someone ☐

5. Gossiping about someone ☐

6. Being happy to help if someone asks ☐

7. Refusing to share your sweets ☐

8. Joining in with being unkind to someone, even when you can see it's upsetting them ☐

9. Being honest when it might seem easier not to tell the truth ☐

10. Being prepared to tell someone you believe in God ☐

Answers on page 109.

In Naaman's household it would have been the servant girl's job to do exactly as she was told – along with all the other servants. But she could choose to do her work without complaining.

ARE YOU UP FOR A CHALLENGE? This week, don't wait to be asked to do things at home or at school – just go ahead and do them, and do them cheerfully! When we help each other with a smile on our face, it makes God smile too.

Have a think now, then use this space to make a list of helpful things you could do. If you can come up with at least seven, that's one for every day of the week!

Not only was the servant girl brave enough to tell Naaman's wife that Naaman needed to go to Elisha the prophet – she also had hero-strength trust in God that He would make Naaman better. It never even entered her head that He wouldn't.

And, of course, God did.

Naaman was given God's instructions: 'Go down to the River Jordan and dip yourself in it seven times.'

Naaman didn't like the sound of that, but his servants persuaded him it was worth a try.

Six times Naaman ducked down into the dirty river water; six times he bobbed up again, still with his skin disease. But on the seventh time? Up he came, and his skin was smooth and clear and totally healed!

Three cheers for **NAAMAN'S SERVANT,** our **HERO NUMBER 2!**

She wasn't afraid to speak up for God. And because she did, Naaman came to know the one true God, who made him all better.

Even though the Bible doesn't mention her name, God knows who this girl was. He knows everything about her, and loved her obedience to Him. We don't follow Jesus so that we get fame and applause, but we do know that God sees everything we do for Him. That's got to be worth it!

Why not say this prayer to God now?

Thank You, God, for the hero servant girl who showed Naaman exactly who You are. Please help me to be brave enough to talk to other people about You too. Please give me a hero faith to trust You completely, every day and always. Amen.

3 GIDEON
The not-so-scaredy-cat
Read all about him in
JUDGES 6–7

Are you brave? I try to be but sometimes things scare me or make me nervous, like if I have to stand up and talk in front of people!

People can feel scared and nervous for all sorts of reasons. Even if you're usually a brave sort of person, there still might be something that makes you want to run away as fast as you can in the opposite direction.

What scares YOU?

_____

_____

_____

_____

When you're feeling scared, never forget that God is always there for You. Tell Him what's going on. He'll be right beside you every single second.

Do you think a scaredy-cat could ever be a hero? If you don't, then just wait till you hear about a man called Gideon.

God was on the lookout for a hero. His special people, the Israelites, had some enemies. They were from a place called Midian and they made the Israelites' lives miserable. God wasn't going to put up with it anymore. So, He chose someone to rescue them.

But the man God had His eye on for the job wasn't big and tough. The man in God's mind wasn't a great leader who'd won lots of battles. The man God was about to tap on the shoulder – Gideon – wasn't 'important' or brave at all.

In fact, when God found him, he wasn't standing tall and facing up to the enemy – oh, no… He was hiding.

I love the story of Gideon! It reminds me that, no matter who we are or what we do, God sees the hero in us – in me and in you. Fandabulous, huh?

I wish I could have seen Gideon's face when he heard God's message. There he was, cowering away from the enemy in a hole in the ground, when suddenly, from out of nowhere, God's angel turned up and said something amazing. Crack the code to find out what it was!

A	B	C	D	E	F	G	H	I	J	K	L	M
△	◻	◍	▷	▽	▷	⊙	▷	◻	◁	⬚	⊟	⬡

N	O	P	Q	R	S	T	U	V	W	X	Y	Z
⊠	∨	▷	▷	◁	◁⊕	⊡	◁	⬓	⊖	⊞	◁

'⊕▷▽ ⊟∨◁▷ ◻◁ ⊞◻⊕▷ ⊞∨◻,
⊠◁△◁▽ △⊠▷ △◻⊙▷⊕⊞ △△⊠!'

_____

_____

_____

Answer in Judges 6 v 12.

Brave and mighty? Seriously?! Gideon was hiding in a hole!

29

Imagine an angel turning up in your bedroom when you're supposed to be doing your homework (but actually you're messing with your hair) – and calling you 'brave and mighty'!

Draw a picture of what your face would look like (with whatever hairstyle you fancy!).

And what would you do? Tick a choice below or come up with something else.

Scream and run away ☐

Hide under the bed ☐

Pretend you haven't heard a thing and carry on with your homework ☐

Fake being asleep ☐

Feel rather proud of yourself ☐

Something else... ☐

_____

Well, not only did God tell Gideon he was brave and mighty, He also told him to go and rescue His special people from their enemies! So what do you think Gideon did – being a bit of a scaredy-cat?

What Gideon *didn't* do was pat himself on the back and think, 'Finally! I always knew I was a hero.'

No. Gideon argued with God. Just a little bit…

'But, God – I'm nothing. I'm nobody. No one in my family is less important than I am. How can I rescue Your people? I mean, look at me!'

> But the thing about God is, you can't argue with Him. Because God always knows best. So God is always right!

Cross out every v, x and z to read God's answer to Gideon.

'xzvYouvvxzcanzxz xvxdovxzitzxzzbecausezvzlvxzwill zvvxhelpzzxyouvzv.'

Answer in Judges 6 v 16.

That was the moment Gideon knew he had to do what God wanted. That was the moment he knew that if God was asking him to do this, then God would give him everything he needed to succeed.

That was the moment Gideon started acting like a hero! (Although he was probably still quite scared…)

The first thing Gideon did was blow a trumpet to call together an army. You'll never guess how many men came – 32,000! Gideon must have thought, 'Wow! Defeating God's enemies is going to be a piece of cake!' (He probably stopped feeling quite so scared at that point too.)

He might have started to make a list of all the things each soldier in his army was going to need. Stuff like the following ten things. Can you find them in the word search?

HELMET									
SHIELD	R	H	R	S	E	B	Y	B	N	I
FOOD	S	E	O	H	S	D	O	O	G	A
GOOD	Y	L	K	I	A	W	T	T	E	N
SHOES	F	M	T	E	N	T	O	T	M	R
TENT	O	E	S	L	E	H	I	R	I	E
ARMOUR	O	T	E	D	T	C	Y	E	D	T
TORCH	D	R	S	A	R	R	O	N	C	A
WATER	X	A	A	R	M	O	U	R	K	W
BATTLE	E	Y	M	C	R	T	J	Y	O	K
PLAN	B	A	T	T	L	E	P	L	A	N
SWORD										

Answer on page 109.

But God wasn't interested in lists and He certainly didn't care about a huge army. All God wanted was for Gideon to learn to trust Him. So what did God do? He told Gideon to send most of those 32,000 men away!

You see, with 32,000 men, Gideon might have felt he didn't need God's help to rescue His people from their enemies. He might have thought he and his army were strong enough and powerful enough on their own, without God having to do a thing.

But God wanted to show Gideon, his men and the enemy, just how powerful He really was.

God also wanted Gideon to learn that He will give us everything we need to cope in scary situations. **_OUR JOB ISN'T TO STRUGGLE AND TRY TO DEAL WITH DIFFICULT THINGS ON OUR OWN. OUR JOB IS TO TRUST GOD._**

Gideon was just about to find this out.

So – how many men do you think God wanted in Gideon's army? Before you turn the page, have a guess...

☐ 30,000   ☐ 20,000
☐ 1,500   ☐ 950
☐ 700   ☐ 300

What was your guess? If you thought 300, you're spot on!

Now, remember the face you drew on page 30? Well, imagine how Gideon must have felt when he realised he now only had 300 men to defeat the enemy army. Draw what his face might have looked like here.

But Gideon *didn't* run away. He waited for God to tell him what to do next. He was learning that the only thing he could do was trust God. And God, who knew Gideon inside out and understood that he was a bit of a scaredy-cat, didn't let him down. He gave Gideon exactly what he needed.

That night, God told Gideon to go to the enemy camp and listen to what the soldiers there were saying. Gideon heard one of them telling another about a dream he'd had.

Here's what the other soldier said – use a mirror to read it for yourself!

Midian and our whole army!' 'God has given him victory over

Answer in Judges 7 v 14.

Wow! God had shown His enemies in a dream that they weren't going to win against Gideon. God was in charge!

Gideon followed God's plan exactly. He gave each soldier a trumpet and a stone jar with a torch inside. Then he told his men to copy what he did.

Outside the enemy camp, first he blew his trumpet. Then he threw his jar on the ground so that it smashed with a huge crash. Then he waved his burning torch in the air and shouted, 'For the LORD and for Gideon!'

And everything Gideon did, his men did too. In fact, they made such a noise and kerfuffle that now it was the enemy soldiers' turn to be scaredy-cats – they woke up screaming and ran off into the night!

Gideon may not have been the bravest soldier or the greatest leader. But God still chose him to rescue His people. God wanted to teach him (and us!) how powerful He is. He wanted to show Gideon that, no matter how hard or scary things were, He was with him.

GIDEON is our **HERO NUMBER 3** because, in the end, he made a hero's choice: he chose to trust and obey God. What God wanted him to face was terrifying. But with God's strength, he did face it – and he won.

Look back to page 27 and read through the list you wrote of things that scare you. Then pray this prayer...

Thank You, God, for everything I can learn from the story of Gideon. Thank You for proving to scaredy-cat Gideon that You were with him and would never let him down. Please take all my worries and fears now, God. Help me to really know, deep inside, that You are with me. Amen.

4
RAHAB
God's unlikely hero
Read all about her in *JOSHUA 1–2*

When you think of a superhero, what comes into your mind? Do you imagine:

- **Someone flying through the air with a cape streaming out behind them?**

- **Someone in a mask so their identity isn't discovered while they're doing their superhero bit?**

- **Someone with incredible super-strength?**

- **Someone who's just... well... indestructible?**

Draw a picture of the superhero you can see in your head right now!

If you were a superhero, what super-special abilities would you like to have? My top super power would be the ability to breathe underwater!

How about you? See if you can come up with your top five super powers. Write them here.

1. _____

2. _____

3. _____

4. _____

5. _____

If I was a breathing-under-water superhero, I'd like to be called 'Wonderfish Boy'! What would your superhero name be? Write it down here.

_____

If you look back at the first three heroes in this book, what do you notice about them? Did they have big muscles or X-ray vision? Did they know they had special abilities that could help them save the world? Did they have a proper superhero uniform that only fitted them?

No… They were ordinary.

There was nothing in particular that made them stand out. They had their strengths, but they had their weaknesses too. Like all of us.

And if anyone had gone up to them and told them they were heroes – they'd probably have laughed!

But, you see, that's what God does. **HE TAKES ORDINARY PEOPLE AND GIVES THEM THE COURAGE TO DO EXTRAORDINARY THINGS FOR HIM!**

Whether that means giving up everything to help someone in need, or seeing off an enemy army, with God's power anything is possible! All we have to do is trust Him and say, 'Yes, God' – and God will do the rest.

Our next hero was someone else mega-ordinary, who became someone super-brave for God. Her name was Rahab and she lived in a city called Jericho.

Rahab found herself right slap bang in the middle of God's plans for His special people, the Israelites!

God wanted the Israelites to settle in the land He'd chosen for them – the land of Canaan. They would have a good life there. They'd be comfortable with plenty to eat.

The trouble was, there were people living in Canaan already. People who didn't want to know God. People who wanted to live their lives their own way and leave Him out. Those people didn't like the Israelites, so the Israelites would have to be very careful when they started to move in.

Do you know the name of the man God chose to lead His people into Canaan?

Write out the letters below in the correct number order to find out!

The first thing Joshua did was to send two spies into Canaan. He wanted to know more about the place so that he could work out the best way to get God's people there safely.

Being a spy was a dangerous job! If they were caught, they'd be in BIG trouble. So, who would help them in a place that was full of their enemies?

Rahab, that's who!

Rahab let the two spies hide in her house.

This was a HUGE thing for Rahab to do. If anyone found out that she had Israelite spies staying at her house, she'd be in just as much trouble as the spies. Still, as long as no one knew they were there...

But, oh no... Someone *did* know they were there. Someone who ran and told the king of Jericho they were there! And the king of Jericho sent his men straight round to Rahab's house to arrest them.

BANG! BANG! BANG!

How do you think Rahab must have felt when she heard the king's men thumping on her door?

How would YOU have felt? Write down a few words to describe those feelings here.

_____

_____

When the spies heard the 'BANG BANG BANG', they probably didn't feel too good either. They must have thought they had no hope. And when the king's men growled at Rahab, 'You've got enemy spies in your house! Bring them out here now!', they must have thought they'd had it.

But Rahab had other ideas. Rahab wanted to be on God's side. So, Rahab had hidden the spies to help God's people. Can you guess where?

Look at the picture of Rahab's house and see if you can find them. But when you do – ssshh! – don't tell anyone! It's top secret!

Now, with the spies safely out of sight, what do you think Rahab said to the king's men? Read the words in the read-around to find out.

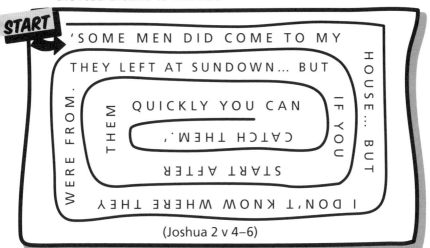

START

'SOME MEN DID COME TO MY HOUSE... BUT THEY LEFT AT SUNDOWN... BUT I DON'T KNOW WHERE THEY WERE FROM. START AFTER THEM QUICKLY YOU CAN CATCH THEM.'

(Joshua 2 v 4–6)

Talk about being a hero! Not only did Rahab find a really good hiding place for the spies, she also came up with a good enough story so that the king's men didn't even search her house.

Read the following questions and answer by ticking 'yes' or 'no'.

Do you think Rahab was afraid when she hid the spies? YES ☐ NO ☐

Do you think Rahab was nervous about lying to the king? YES ☐ NO ☐

Do you think Rahab had made up her mind to trust God? YES ☐ NO ☐

When the king's men had left, the spies must have wondered why Rahab had gone to so much trouble to help them. She wasn't even an Israelite!

Rahab cleared that up right away. She said to them: 'The Lord your God is God in heaven above and here on earth' (Joshua 2 v 11).

Rahab knew exactly who God was. She also knew how scared everyone in Canaan was of Him. They had heard all about His great power and knew they could never win against Him. They knew God would give the land of Canaan to the Israelites – but they wouldn't turn to Him.

But Rahab knew that she needed God to protect her, and she wanted to be sure that she and her family would be safe.

So, did the spies agree to help Rahab? Crack the code and write out the words to see what they said.

'⬜∇ ▷◁∇⬜◁∇ ⊞∨⬜ ⊕▷⋀⊕ ⬜▷∇⊠ ⊕▷∇ ⊟∨◁▷ ⦿⬜◁∇◁ ▫◁ ⊕▷▫◁ ⊟⋀⊠▷, ⬜∇ ⬜⬜⊟⊟ ⊕◁∇⋀⊕ ⊞∨⬜ ⬜∇⊟⊟.'

_____

_____

_____

_____

A	B	C	D	E	F	G	H	I	J	K	L	M
⋀	⬇	⬆	▷	∇	▷	⦿	▷	⬜	◁	⬇	⊟	⋀

N	O	P	Q	R	S	T	U	V	W	X	Y	Z
⊠	∨	▷	▷	◁	◁	⊕	▫	◁	⬜	⊖	⊞	Z

God wants everyone everywhere to believe and trust in Him, but not because He's proud and boastful and too full of Himself.

God wants us to trust Him and let Him guide us every day **BECAUSE HE LOVES US.** He really does know what is best for us. God doesn't make rules for the sake of rules. He's given us guidelines to keep us safe and help us get the most out of our lives.

And Rahab from Jericho had worked that out!

Write the back-to-front words the right way round to see what made ordinary Rahab such an extraordinary hero for God.

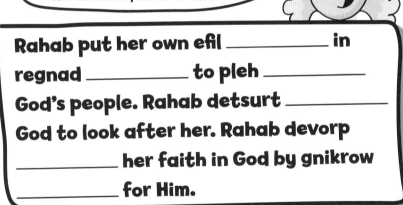

Rahab put her own efil _____ in regnad _____ to pleh _____ God's people. Rahab detsurt _____ God to look after her. Rahab devorp _____ her faith in God by gnikrow _____ for Him.

Answers on page 110.

But that's not the end of Rahab's story!

God did look after her. The spies told her to tie a red rope to her window. Then, when Joshua led the Israelites into Jericho, that would be a signal for them. They would leave the people inside that house – Rahab and her family – alone.

God did more than just look after Rahab. Because she was so faithful to Him, **HE WELCOMED HER INTO HIS FAMILY** – in a really big way!

Remember Ruth, our hero number 1? Ruth married Boaz and together they had a son they called Obed, who became an ancestor of David and eventually Jesus.

Well, guess who Boaz's mum was? YES – RAHAB!

God kept Rahab safe, and He honoured her in the most amazing way! He gave her a place in the family line leading to Jesus!

God could see the hero in **RAHAB.** So can we – that's why she deserves to be our **HERO NUMBER 4!**

Talk to God now...

God, I praise You for Rahab and for her inspiring story! She wasn't rich or famous or powerful – she was just ordinary, and her own people wanted nothing to do with You. But because Rahab trusted You, she became Your unlikely hero. You gave her all the super powers she needed to be a hero for You. I want to be on Your side, God, just like Rahab. Please help me to listen to You and to follow You every day – and to truly believe that I am special to You. Thank You for loving me and taking care of me. Amen.

5 ABIGAIL

The peacemaker

Read all about her in *1 SAMUEL 25*

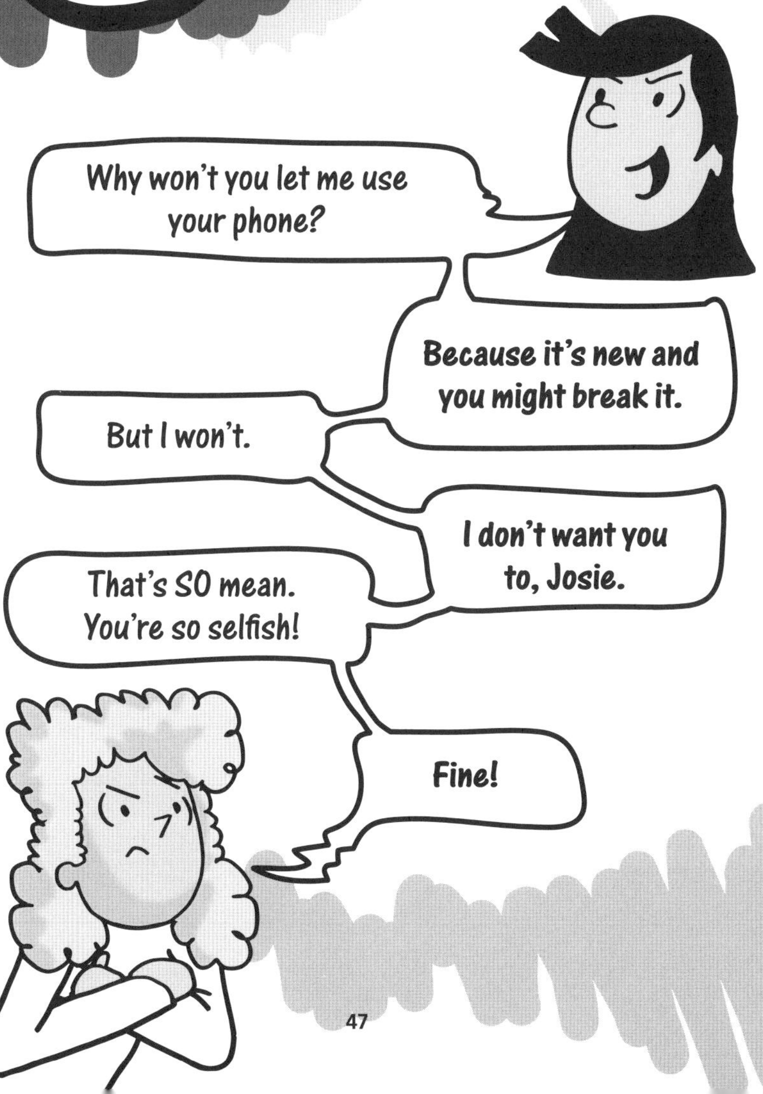

Arguing with someone is horrible, isn't it? And it can lead to lots more horribleness:

- **Saying nasty things you don't really mean**
- **Breaking up friendships**
- **Spreading lies**
- **Feeling hurt**
- **Feeling sad**
- **Wanting to get your own back**
- **Feeling and being grumpy**

AND ARGUMENTS CAN SOMETIMES START OVER SOMETHING REALLY SMALL AND STUPID.

On top of that, if you've argued with someone and haven't made it up, it can get in the way of your friendship with God.

You might stop talking to God because you feel bad inside and think He won't want to hear from you. Then, if you don't say sorry to God and ask Him to help you deal with the argument, it can take a lot, lot longer to sort things out.

If an argument's really bad, it can help to chat to someone else about it. Our youth leader at church, Greg – he's stonking at sorting out arguments. He just has this way of calming everyone down.

Our hero number 5 was so good at sorting out arguments that she ended up saving people's lives. Abigail was married to a man called Nabal. And they were total opposites.

Look at these words and draw a line from each one to join it with its exact opposite.

Proud	**Difficult**
Happy	**Exciting**
Selfish	**Slow**
Easy	**Generous**
Fast	**Noisy**
Quiet	**Humble**
Boring	**Sad**

Answers on page 110.

Well, Nabal was selfish, rude, proud and very foolish – but Abigail was kind, thoughtful, humble and very wise. She also didn't waste time when something needed to be done.

Which, as it turns out, was just as well for Nabal…

A man called David would one day be a very important king. But at the time he met Abigail, he was running away from another king – Saul.

King Saul was jealous of David and wanted to kill him. So David had to hide away from him with his trusty band of soldiers.

One of the hiding places David found was on land that belonged to Nabal. Although he could have done, David never stole a thing from Nabal. But there were plenty of other thieves around. So, while David and his men were there, David made sure the workers and the animals were safe.

One day, David sent some of his men to ask Nabal for some food and supplies. After all, he had been protecting Nabal's land and herds.

But what did Nabal do?

Nabal was very, very stupid. He was rude and selfish too. He wouldn't give anything to David or his men – and he caused a HUGE argument.

Oops! When David heard what Nabal had said, he was hopping mad. No one talked to him like that and got away with it!

David told his men to get their weapons ready for a fight. He wasn't just after Nabal now. He was after everyone who worked for him too.

This trouble was BIG. David meant business, but how could he be stopped? How could things be made right again? Who do you turn to for help when it's all as bad as this?

> Easy... You turn to a hero, that's who!

If anyone could sort this out, it was Abigail. Nabal didn't even know or care that he'd made David so angry! But Abigail found out what had happened through a servant.

Abigail wasn't like her husband. She was good and wise – not like foolish, grumpy Nabal!

How do you think Nabal might have reacted if the servant had gone to talk to him instead of to Abigail?

Put a tick next to the true sentences, and a cross next to the false ones.

1. Nabal would have hugged the servant. ☐

2. Nabal would have sent the servant away grumpily. ☐

3. Nabal would have rudely ignored what the servant said. ☐

4. Nabal would have asked the servant to say sorry to David. ☐

Answers on page 110.

I think Abigail was used to sorting out Nabal's arguments. When the servant told her what had happened, she didn't ask Nabal for advice. She didn't have to stop and think what to do. She just got on and did it. Abigail seemed to know how to sort things out, just like that. You see? Wise...

Some people are really good at being peacemakers. When you fall out with someone, who do you go to in order to get help with sorting things out?

_____

Just imagine for a minute...

Two of your friends have fallen out with each other. It's bad. They won't speak to each other. They won't say sorry. When they're in the same room, they won't even look at each other!

Now, imagine that another of your friends says to you, 'Please, you have to help...'

Have a think about what you could say to your two friends. Could you...

- **Ask them to tell you what the problem really is?**

- **Encourage them to see the problem from each other's point of view?**

- **Help them to try saying sorry for being cross?**

- **See if they will at least start to talk to each other?**

It may be hard to come up with what you might say, but have a go – and write down a few thoughts here.

_____

_____

_____

_____

_____

_____

_____

_____

_____

Abigail packed up gifts for David and his men – a lot of gifts! Plenty of food to eat and plenty to drink. This is what David had asked for, but Abigail was very generous. She was also very humble.

When Abigail met David, she didn't just bow. She threw herself flat out on the ground in front of him. Even though this muddle had nothing to do with her, she asked David to blame her and not her husband.

'If only I'd been at home when your men arrived,' she said, 'none of it would have happened. I would have taken care of everything instead of Nabal being so mean and rude.'

And Abigail asked David to forgive her.

But there was something else Abigail said. Something that showed her closeness to God, and exactly how wise she really was!

Abigail said to David: 'One day, God will make you king of Israel. He will keep you safe and do lots of good things for you. Don't get your own back on Nabal now by attacking him and his men. If you do, you'll always remember it and you'll always feel bad.'

What a hero peacemaker!

David said thank you to Abigail for being so sensible. Then he told her to go home. He had listened to her and he wouldn't hurt anyone.

So, not only did Abigail save her husband's life (and her own and all their workers!) – she was also incredibly brave. Brave enough to speak up and stop David from doing something he would only feel sorry for later. Something that would have got in the way of his friendship with God.

How wise and caring is that?

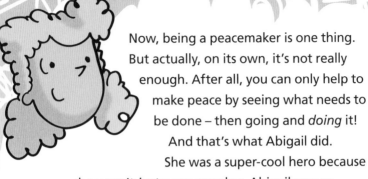

Now, being a peacemaker is one thing. But actually, on its own, it's not really enough. After all, you can only help to make peace by seeing what needs to be done – then going and *doing* it! And that's what Abigail did.

She was a super-cool hero because she wasn't *just* a peacemaker. Abigail was an…

(Trace over the letters and why not colour them in too – bold and bright like Abigail!)

ACTION HERO!

So that's our **HERO NUMBER 5, ABIGAIL!** Why not say this prayer now?

Wow, God! Abigail, the action hero! When there was a bad argument, she didn't stand by and do nothing. Even when it wasn't her fault, she set out to put things right with her whole heart. Abigail knew what You wanted, God, and she served You to make it happen. Please help me to serve You like that too. And teach me to be a peacemaker. Amen.

6

PETER
Full of potential
Read all about him in **MATTHEW 14**

To find our hero number 6, Peter, let's jump forward in the Bible to the New Testament.

Peter was one of Jesus' disciples. More than that, he was one of the first four men Jesus chose to follow Him and be a part of His special team of 12. That has to give Peter a bit of a wow factor to start with!

Before he met Jesus, Peter already had a full-time job. That's the job he knew and he worked hard at it. He probably never imagined his life would be any different.

Crack the code to work out what Peter's job was.

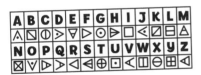

Answer on page 110.

But then along came Jesus, walking beside the lake where Peter was working. And, suddenly, nothing would ever be the same.

When Jesus asked Peter to follow Him, Peter didn't have to think twice. He just dropped his fishing nets right there and then – and went with Jesus.

Of course, Peter would have had no idea what he was letting himself in for. But Jesus saw something in him right from the very start. He saw that this down-to-earth, hard-working fisherman had **THE POTENTIAL TO BE A HERO.**

And Peter did some amazing things for Jesus! But he also made a lot of mistakes…

I think that's what I like about Peter the most. He loved Jesus and wanted to do his absolute best for Him. But he was human – so he messed up sometimes. And Jesus forgave him and kept him in His gang anyway. Here's three questions for you!

1. Do you love Jesus? YES ☐ NO ☐

2. Do you sometimes get things wrong – do things Jesus wouldn't want you to do or say things He wouldn't want you to say? YES ☐ NO ☐

3. Do you ever worry that Jesus won't forgive you? YES ☐ NO ☐

If you answered 'YES' to those three questions, then
YOU'RE JUST LIKE PETER!

Even if we love Jesus a LOT – and I do! – we're still probably going to make mistakes sometimes.

But if we don't tell Jesus we're sorry for the wrong things we do, and just ignore Him and keep on doing them – that's what gets in the way of our friendship with Him. So, whatever mistakes you've made, and whatever you get wrong in the future, always remember these four things (write the words in the right order).

Jesus to sorry Say

_____

not to hard do again it Try

_____

it Really mean

_____

Jesus you Know forgives that

_____

Answers on page 110.

Peter is written about quite a few times in the Gospels, and in the book of Acts that comes right after them.

One story tells how, on a stormy night, Jesus' disciples were sailing across a lake. Their boat was being thrown about on the rough waves. It was hard work keeping it afloat.

Jesus wasn't with His friends. He'd stayed behind to spend some time on His own talking to God.

When He'd finished, He went to meet them on their boat.

But the way Jesus did that was to **WALK ON THE WATER!**

When the disciples saw Jesus walking on the water, they thought they were seeing a ghost! But then Jesus called out to them.

Peter was the only one brave enough to speak to Him.

Follow the arrows and write down the words in the correct order to read what Peter said.

'if Lord, is it you really, me order come to on out water the you to.'

_____

_____

_____

Answer in Matthew 14 v 28.

Remember, there's a storm going on. The wind would have been roaring and the waves heaving. What on earth made Peter think getting out of the boat was a good idea?! And when Jesus said, 'All right, then, Peter, come on!' what made him bold enough to actually do it?

FAITH — THAT'S WHAT.

Draw Peter walking on the water to Jesus.

How do you think Peter would have felt? Excited? Nervous? He had left a safe place (the boat) to step into a dangerous place (the stormy water)!

But Peter could see Jesus. He was learning that Jesus was his safe place. He believed Jesus would look after him.

For a moment, Peter had hero faith… until he suddenly got scared.

I find it hard to stay focused sometimes. I get distracted at school all the time! Especially if my tummy's rumbling... I won't learn a thing!

Getting distracted can be a problem. It can even be dangerous, especially if you stop concentrating when you're doing something like crossing a road!

What Peter stopped concentrating on was Jesus.

What distracts you from Jesus?

- **Things you worry about?**
- **Things people say who don't believe in Jesus?**
- **A bad mood?**

Write a few things down here.

Well, one minute, there Peter was, walking on water, his eyes fixed firmly on Jesus – the next, he'd gone all wobbly!

He started listening to the rushing wind. He started looking at the wild waves. He stopped believing that Jesus – who had invited him out of the boat – would help him.

Peter's hero faith turned into zero faith, and guess what happened? **HE BEGAN TO SINK!**

Peter's faith wasn't strong enough right at that moment to believe in this awesome water-walking miracle. But he did cry out to Jesus to help him. And the second he did that, Jesus reached out, took hold of him, and helped him back into the boat.

'Why did you doubt me, Peter?' Jesus asked.

Putting our faith in Jesus – trusting Him completely – isn't easy for us. Jesus knows that. And He didn't turn His back on Peter because Peter had a wobble.

He won't turn His back on us either.

Look again at the things you wrote down that distract you from Jesus. Why not ask Him to help you deal with them right now?

Call out to Jesus, just like Peter did.

Now, you may be asking, 'Hang on a minute – why does Peter *not* having enough faith make him a Topz 10 Bible hero?' Well, being a hero doesn't mean you're perfect. Peter wasn't perfect. None of us is perfect – except Jesus!

But what Peter teaches us is that, even though we're not perfect, we've got to keep going. Peter didn't say to himself, 'My faith is never going to be good enough – *I'm* never going to be good enough – so I may as well give up.'

No! Unjumble these words and write them out in the correct order to see what Peter did.

He learning on kept

_____

trying on kept He

_____

with stuck Jesus He

_____

Answers on page 110.

There's a big word that means sticking with something, no matter what. Here it is but all the letter 'E's are missing. Fill them in and read out the word.

P __ R S __ V __ R A N C __

Peter was still getting it wrong, even right near the end of Jesus' life. When Jesus got arrested, Peter got scared that people would be after him too. So he denied that he knew Jesus at all. When Peter realised what he'd done, he felt so terrible that he ran away.

But that wasn't the end for Peter and Jesus!

After Jesus died and came back to life, He appeared to His disciples lots of times – including to Peter.

JESUS DIDN'T LEAVE PETER OUT.

In fact, He gave him more work to do. Jesus wanted Peter to get out there and tell people all about Him so that they could be friends with Him too, and with His Father God.

Peter made mistakes. He let Jesus down. But in the end, he became someone really important in spreading the news of Jesus around the world.

So, can you see why **PETER** is our

HERO NUMBER 6?

Why not pray this prayer now?

> *Jesus, Peter knew he was far from perfect and so did You. But You never gave up on him and he never gave up on You. I'm sorry for when I get things wrong. Please help me to be like Peter – and pick myself up and keep on trying. Amen.*

7 DEBORAH
The straight-talker
Read all about her in *JUDGES 4–5*

Now that you've read about quite a few heroes from the Bible, you're probably starting to think that you have to be super-human to be a hero for God.

But that's just not true! In fact, what made these people so heroic was that they were so...

ORDINARY!

That's right – none of God's heroes started out being super-human. They were just ordinary people, like us.

What they did do was learn to trust God in a heroic way. That's why God was able to use them and do good things for them – and **TURN THEIR ORDINARY LIVES INTO EXTRAORDINARY HERO LIVES!**

Life with God is actually full of challenges.

Being the people God wants us to be – living the way He wants us to live – none of it's easy. But God knows that. That's why He's always on hand to help us out.

Our job is to stay close to Him. Then we can keep in touch with Him about what's right and what's wrong, and the choices we often have to make. Here are a few everyday choices. Put a tick in the box for God's choices, and a cross for those that aren't His way of doing things:

Here are a few everyday choices. Put a tick in the box for God's choices, and a cross for those that aren't His way of doing things.

1. I could help Mum put the shopping away, but I'd rather play on my Xbox. ☐

2. There's a new kid in my class. I'll invite them round after school to help them settle in. ☐

3. My friend's really wound me up. I'm never speaking to her again. ☐

4. I can't be bothered to do my homework. I'll tell my teacher I couldn't do it because I was ill. ☐

5. I could pinch one of my cousin's sweets, but I'll ask if it would be all right to have one instead. ☐

6. I'm supposed to be going out, but my sister's feeling upset. So I'll stay at home and play her favourite games with her to cheer her up. ☐

In the Old Testament part of the Bible, there's a book called Judges.

Judges in the Old Testament were a bit different to the kind of judge we see in courts of law today. They did sometimes help people decide what was right and what was wrong. But, when God's special people, the Israelites, ended up in trouble because they'd stopped obeying God, often judges led armies to help rescue them from their enemies too.

Our hero number 7 was one of God's judges. Her name was Deborah. Not only was Deborah a judge – she was also a prophet. So, she helped the Israelites make important decisions, and she gave them messages from God as well.

Even though Deborah was wise and important, she made it really easy for God's people to come and talk to her. The Bible says she just used to sit outside under a palm tree, waiting for them!

One day, Deborah had a message from God for a man called Barak. So she sent for Barak to tell him what God wanted him to do.

You can see Deborah sitting under her palm tree below. Help Barak to get to her as quickly as possible by finding the right path through the maze.

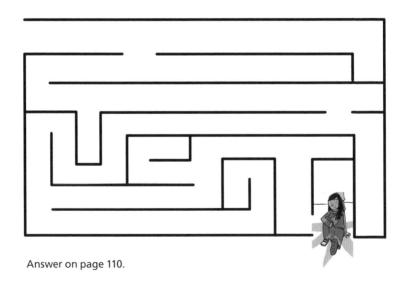

Answer on page 110.

About 20 years before Deborah was a judge, God's people had turned away from God (which they kept on doing!). So nasty King Jabin had got hold of them and made them his slaves.

This king wasn't nice to them at all. Neither was the head of his army, Sisera. But now God's people had told God they were sorry. They'd called out for His help. And God was about to give it to them.

Well, Deborah wasn't a ditherer. **IF GOD TOLD HER TO DO SOMETHING, SHE DID IT.** No arguments.

When God told her to tell Barak to go after Sisera and King Jabin's army with 10,000 men – that's exactly what Deborah did.

She told Barak, 'Sisera may have a huge army and 900 chariots, but it's not a problem. God is going to let you win against them.'

The trouble was, Barak didn't have Deborah's hero faith. Even though winning was a promise from God, he wasn't at all sure it would happen.

Draw Barak's face when he heard what God wanted him to do.

In the end, Barak did go. He got together an army and he set off. But because he was scared, he would only go if one particular person went with him.

   Can you crack the code and write out what Barak said to Deborah?

‘⬡ ⬜⬜⬛⊟ ☉∨ ⬜▷ ⊞∨⊡ ☉∨ ⬜⬜⊕▷
△▽, ⬝⊡⊕ ⬜▷ ⊞∨⊡ ▷∨⬛'⊕ ☉∨
⬜⬜⊕▷ △▽, ⬡ ⬜∨⬛'⊕ ☉∨ ▽⬜⊕▷△◁.'

_____

_____

_____

Answer in Judges 4 v 8.

It's not really surprising that Barak was scared to go and face Sisera. And it showed just how much respect he had for Deborah that he'd only go if she went too.

   Maybe he thought it would be easier to trust in God's promise if Deborah agreed to go with him. It would show him that Deborah had no doubts that God meant what He said.

   When we have to do something scary, there's nothing wrong with asking someone to go with us. Sometimes we call it having 'moral support'. But Barak trusted Deborah more than he trusted God on His own. And that's not what God wants us to do.

There was nothing fake about Deborah. She didn't dish out advice and messages, pretending they were from God, just so that she could be a celebrity.

DEBORAH BELIEVED IN GOD, THROUGH AND THROUGH. She had no doubts about Him at all. When Barak said, 'Come with me,' Deborah didn't even have to stop and think.

'All right,' she said. Just like that!

But that's when her hero straight-talking kicked in again. Yes, she would go. But because Barak hadn't trusted God enough, it wouldn't be Barak who would get the credit for the final victory.

He would win – for sure. But he wouldn't be remembered for winning.

The person who would actually be known for beating Sisera **WOULD BE A WOMAN.**

Haha! How's that for a bit of girl power?!

It's no surprise that straight-talking Deborah's straight talk came true – every single word.

The battle against King Jabin was won, and it was a woman who got rid of Sisera himself. Her name was Jael.

Deborah had given her life to God. She wasn't afraid to tell others what He said. She wasn't even scared to head into a battlefield, because God had promised that His people would win.

Deborah wasn't just a hero prophet. **SHE HAD HERO COURAGE AND FAITH TOO.**

Being as faithful as Deborah is hard. All sorts of things can get in our way – fear, doubt, worry.

Just try to keep holding on to God, and remember Deborah's advice. Colour in the dotted shapes to see what it is.

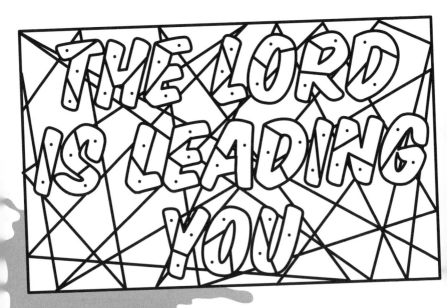

Knowing that God is leading us really can help us feel bold, just like Deborah! It's God who gives us that hero courage.

How courageous do you feel? Have a think about the parts of your life where you feel boldest, and where you'd like to feel a little braver (with God's help!). Then write down your thoughts here.

I feel courageous when...

_____

_____

_____

_____

I would like more courage for...

_____

_____

_____

_____

I still love playdough. You can make anything with it – cars, houses, spaceships, sea ships, aeroplanes, animals, monsters...

Well, did you know that anyone can be a hero for God? Anyone – who's ready and willing to let God mould them like playdough!

God wants to form us, shape us, and smooth out all the rough edges. He wants us to say, 'Yes, God. I'm ready for You!'

WHEN WE CHOOSE TO LET GOD GUIDE US AND CHANGE US – THAT'S WHEN WE CAN START TO BE HEROES FOR HIM.

That's what our **HERO NUMBER 7, DEBORAH,** did. And God used her to help rescue His people.

Just think what He might have in store for you...

Why not talk to him now?

God, I'm amazed by Deborah and her hero heart. I want faith and courage just like hers. Help me to throw myself into Your adventures, and not to be scared of them. Thank You for always going ahead of me to show me the way. Amen.

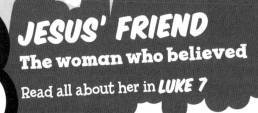

8

JESUS' FRIEND
The woman who believed
Read all about her in **LUKE 7**

Jesus is amazingly, unbelievably, incredibly wonderful! He was perfect when He lived on the earth and He's perfect now!

Do you ever stop to have a really good think about what Jesus has done for all of us?

Jesus loves us so much that He came to earth to die instead of us, so that we could live with God forever.

You see, the things we do wrong spoil our friendship with God and make Him sad. Really, those wrong things should mean that *we* die and don't get to be with God at all. But that's not God's plan… because **JESUS DIED INSTEAD OF US!**

What we do need to do is say sorry to God and ask Jesus to come and share our lives. Then, when we do that – and really mean it – we can be God's friends and part of His family ALWAYS!

Jesus died for you. Just think about that for a moment…

Who do you admire? Do you have a favourite sportsperson or actor or singer? Or maybe an author whose books you just can't wait to get your hands on? Choose a favourite person and write their name down here.

_____

Now, imagine you've got the chance to meet that person face-to-face! What would you want to say to them? What could you do for them to show them how important they are to you? Come up with some ideas and make a list.

_____

_____

_____

_____

_____

_____

Amazing! If I was your fave person, I'd be HONOURED!

That's what honouring someone is! It's letting them know:

- **How much they mean to you**
- **How important they are in your life**
- **How special you think they are**
- **How much you think they deserve your time and effort!**

That's how our hero number 8 felt about Jesus.

Hero number 8 obviously had a name, but the Bible doesn't tell us what it was. In fact, it doesn't tell us much about her at all. What it *does* tell us is that this woman who went to visit Jesus did everything RIGHT!

Jesus had gone to have dinner with a man called Simon. Simon was a Pharisee. The Pharisees believed they were good enough for God because they followed rules and did certain things in certain ways. And if people didn't follow their rules and the laws they made up, the Pharisees looked down their noses at them.

Simon the Pharisee was just like the other Pharisees. He was proud. He thought he was better than people who didn't follow the rules.

The woman in the story went to visit Jesus while He was at Simon's house. She hadn't been invited, but she went anyway. She knew Jesus was there and she just had to see Him.

BUT THIS WOMAN WASN'T THE SORT OF PERSON SIMON WOULD WANT IN HIS HOUSE.

She'd done lots of things wrong. People in the town knew about all the things she'd done wrong too.

Simon probably wasn't the only one to look down his nose at her.

There's a word the Bible uses that means 'full of wrong things'. Trace over the dotted letters to find out what it is...

SINFUL

It wasn't just other people who knew the woman was 'sinful'. The woman knew it herself. That was the whole reason why she'd gone to see Jesus. **SHE KNEW SHE NEEDED GOD TO FORGIVE HER.**

How do you think Simon the Pharisee would have felt when she stepped through his doorway? Draw a circle round the feelings he might have had.

Bored   Put out   Not bothered

Delighted   Disgusted   Annoyed

Insulted   Amused

Pleased   Outraged

Answers on page 111.

Simon would have been even more annoyed as he watched what the woman did. She went straight to Jesus. She was so overcome at seeing Him that she started to cry. Her tears fell on His bare feet and she used her long hair to wipe them dry. Then, she kissed Jesus' feet and poured perfume over them.

All this might sound a bit weird to us! But back then, people wore open sandals, or maybe no shoes at all. Their feet got very dirty as they walked around. If you visited someone, a servant would wash your feet for you, so you'd feel clean and comfy. It was polite.

But when Jesus arrived at Simon's house, no one washed His feet. No one gave Him a warm welcome. Simon just proudly got on with thinking what a good person he was!

But the woman, who knew she wasn't good at all, washed Jesus' feet with her own tears. Then she bathed them in perfume that had probably cost her a lot of money.

And let's not forget that she'd gone to Simon's house, where she knew she wasn't welcome, so that she could do it!

Simon was full of pride. The woman was the exact opposite: full of **HERO HUMILITY.**

Nothing mattered to her more than showing Jesus how sorry she was for the things she had done wrong, and how special He was to her.

The difference between Simon and the woman was that... (Unscramble the words and write them out underneath.)

eTh nwmao wken hse dedene d'soG ssenrofevig, tub monSi outhtgh eh asw ydalear ctferep.

_____

_____

_____

Answer on page 111.

Simon's feelings in this story were all very negative. But look at the picture of the woman here and imagine the mixture of feelings *she* would have had as she washed Jesus' feet. Now use the space on the page around her to write those different feelings down.

Remember how much God loves you and wants to be your best friend – then tick your answer for each of the following questions.

1. When you say sorry, God...

A. Sometimes listens
B. Always listens
C. Never listens

2. God loves you...

A. Only when He feels like it
B. All the time, always
C. Only if you do good things

3. God's love...

A. Is always the same
B. Changes with the weather
C. Depends on His mood

4. God will never:

A. Forgive you if you don't go to church
B. Have you in His family if you keep getting things wrong
C. Give up on you or leave you

Answers on page 111.

If the woman in the story had answered those questions, we reckon she would have ticked the right box for every single one. She understood that God loved her and wanted to be her friend. She went to Jesus because:

- **She had hero humility and knew how much she needed Him**

- **She wanted to honour Him the best way she could**

- **She believed that God could forgive her so that she could live a brand-new life**

But Simon didn't think he needed Jesus at all. He thought he was 'good enough' already.

When Simon saw the woman, he couldn't understand how Jesus could let her near Him. After all, she was 'sinful'.

Simon obeyed rules, but he didn't understand that Jesus came to help people just like this woman; that God doesn't turn His back on people. He wants everyone to know Him.

Jesus didn't look down His nose at people who did wrong things. Through Him, God forgave them.

Then they could be God's friends forever.

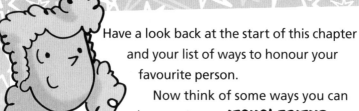

Have a look back at the start of this chapter and your list of ways to honour your favourite person.

Now think of some ways you can honour Jesus. **JESUS' FRIEND,** our **HERO NUMBER 8** was able to honour Him face-to-face. We can honour Him with the way we live our lives.

HOW WILL YOU LIVE YOURS?

Why not talk to Jesus now? Say thank You to Him for everything He has done for you. Then ask Him what you can do for Him. Use this space to write your prayer, and speak it out to Jesus.

_____

_____

_____

_____

_____

_____

_____

Are you the sort of person who has lots of friends, or do you like to stick with just a few? And how well do you know them?

Here's a list of Josie's friends from the Gang. They know each other really well! So, next to each name is a word that she thinks describes them.

Danny	daring
Paul	brainy
Sarah	caring
John	helpful (although Sarah might not think so!)
Dave	sporty
Benny	stonking!

How do you think the rest of the Gang would describe me?

I think you're funny... talented... my best friend!

Time for a challenge!

Come up with a list of friends you think you know really well – you can include cousins and brothers and sisters if you want to. Write down their names, then next to each one, write a word that you feel describes them brilliantly.

Your friends sound as cool as mine!

There are lots of stories in the Bible about friends – people who were great friends to each other, and people who were amazing friends of God.

And, of course, the Bible is all about God, and **HE WANTS TO BE EVERYONE'S FRIEND!**

The books of 1 and 2 Samuel in the Bible aren't *just* about a man called Samuel. You'll also read about David, who was Israel's most famous king. David was hand-picked by God to be king number 2, when king number 1, Saul, let God down rather badly.

But it might surprise you to hear that our hero number 9 isn't actually David. Number 9 is David's very good friend – Jonathan.

Here are some of the things Jonathan was which make him into such a hero friend. But you'll have to unscramble the letters to find out what they are.

nUelsifhs	_____
dniK	_____
evBra	_____
gCinra	_____
estHno	_____
eurT	_____
ingLvo	_____
yalLo	_____
fulthFai	_____

Answers on page 111.

Wow! If I was on the lookout for a new friend, I'd pick Jonathan!

Did you notice the word 'true' in the list of things Jonathan was? You see, it's not just words that can be true. People can be true too.

A true friend is someone who's **A FRIEND THROUGH AND THROUGH.**

• **Nothing can shake them.**

• **Nothing will change how they feel.**

• **Nothing will get in the way of that friendship.**

Jonathan was David's friend to the moon and back – and probably several times round the universe as well!

The following words are all back-to-front. Write them out the correct way round to find out what Jonathan did…

'nahtanoJ erows lanrete pihsdneirf htiw divaD'

_____

_____

_____

Answer in Samuel 18 v 3.

Now, you might be thinking: 'So? Lots of people make good friends. Lots of people *have* good friends who won't let them down.'

But, Jonathan was a hero friend because he kept up his 'eternal friendship' with David, even though he had a very good reason to be jealous and hate him.

You see, Jonathan was the son of king of Israel number 1 – Saul.

Saul was chosen by God to be king. And if Saul had obeyed God and put Him first in everything he did, it should have all worked out. Then the king after Saul would have been Saul's son, Jonathan.

But that's not what happened.

Saul began to like his king's power too much. He started to get too full of his own importance.

King number 1 didn't keep God as his own number 1. So one day, God said, 'I've had enough of this. There will be a new king of Israel.'

The new king would be David.

It was David who would take over from Saul when the time came. Not Jonathan.

So, you can see why Jonathan might have been just a teensy bit jealous…!

Are you starting to get why Jonathan was such an amazing friend now?

Someone else in this story was jealous, though. King Saul! He was SO jealous of David that he tried to kill him – several times!

The trouble was that God's people, the Israelites, loved David more than they loved Saul.

David was a brave leader. He helped God's people win against their enemies. And God's people let Saul know that they thought David was better than he was.

Not only that, Saul also knew that God was on David's side now. So Saul began to hate David.

Draw what King Saul's face might have looked like every time he thought of David.

Now that Jonathan's dad hated David, would that make a difference to how Jonathan felt about his best friend?

Not a chance!

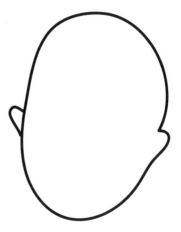

When Jonathan said that his friendship with David would last forever, that's exactly what he meant. You see? **JONATHAN WAS A TRUE FRIEND.**

Even though he would be in big trouble for going against his dad, the king, Jonathan never stopped doing the right thing.

- **He knew his dad was in the wrong.**
- **He stood up for David when his dad said he was going to kill him.**
- **He helped David escape from his dad to keep him safe.**

Standing up for our friends is really important. It shows them that they can trust us because our friendship is true.

When might you need to stand up for someone else?

_____

_____

Standing up for other people can be hard, especially if someone is being teased or bullied. But if someone is being really unkind to one of your friends, or even someone you don't know very well, it's important to try to let them know that you care and you want to help. No one likes to feel that they're all on their own.

If the problem is really bad, you could go with them to talk to a grown-up about it.

And never forget that you can tell God too! He'll want to help you work out the best thing to do – and be brave enough to do it as well.

What kind of friend do you think God would like you to be? Read through this list and tick your answers.

1. **Care more about yourself than about your friend. TRUE ☐ FALSE ☐**

2. **Help out if you understand your homework and your friend doesn't. TRUE ☐ FALSE ☐**

3. **Make time to cheer a friend up if they're feeling down. TRUE ☐ FALSE ☐**

4. **Lie to a friend if it gets you out of trouble. TRUE ☐ FALSE ☐**

5. **Always keep your promises. TRUE ☐ FALSE ☐**

6. **Gossip about a friend if it makes you more popular. TRUE ☐ FALSE ☐**

Answers on page 111.

Jonathan and David's story is an amazing example of the way God wants friendship to be.

But it's also a story about what can happen when someone begins to be jealous of someone else. It shows how hate can start and the sad things that can come from it.

Here's a list of all sorts of different words from this story in the Bible. Can you find them all in the word search?

LOVE
AFFECTION
FRIENDSHIP
PRAISED
HELP
PROMISE
ESCAPE
MADMAN
AFRAID
BATTLE
ENEMY
EVIL

A	F	F	E	C	T	I	O	N	P	O	N
Y	R	A	R	E	A	U	S	K	E	P	H
B	I	S	H	E	B	V	B	R	A	B	E
I	E	S	C	A	P	E	E	A	E	N	L
A	N	N	B	A	E	S	N	R	E	A	P
N	D	P	O	P	I	S	R	M	C	M	A
D	S	T	E	M	T	I	Y	O	N	D	F
I	H	Y	O	N	K	L	O	V	E	A	F
A	I	R	D	L	S	E	L	N	B	M	I
R	P	R	A	I	S	E	D	F	G	H	X
F	E	E	Q	V	E	N	K	L	I	E	J
A	X	B	C	E	L	T	T	A	B	E	N

Answer on page 111.

Jonathan wasn't just a hero friend who ended up saving David's life! He was also a hero for God.

God had a plan for David. He wanted him to be the next king of Israel. And **GOD USED JONATHAN TO HELP KEEP HIS FUTURE KING SAFE.**

It would have been so easy for Jonathan to go along with his dad and let him get rid of David. Much easier than standing up for him!

But Jonathan cared about his friend too much to do that. And he was too sure of right and wrong.

JONATHAN, our **HERO NUMBER 9,** wasn't just a 'good' friend to David. He was a 'God' friend – trustworthy, reliable and true. Always.

Here's a prayer for you to say to God...

God, thank You for teaching me about friendship. Jonathan was such a hero – trustworthy, reliable and true. Just like You. He was exactly the kind of friend You want all of us to be. Please teach me how to be a true friend, God. I want to learn to put other people first, even if that's difficult or not what I feel like doing. I want to be a 'God' friend. Amen.

10

MARTHA
Without a doubt

Read all about her in
LUKE 10 AND JOHN 11

I sometimes have this daydream. Someone
has dropped their bags of shopping, and
I stop to help them pick it up. And that's
when I see! It's someone really, *really* famous!

Once I've helped them put all their
shopping back in their bags, they say,
'Thanks! What would I have done without your
help? You're a life-saver! Hope to see you around.'

Then they walk off with their shopping.

Hope to see you around?!

I can't believe it! A really, properly famous person
just said to me, 'Hope to see you around!'

So anyway, in my daydream, I race off to meet
the Gang...

'Where have you been?' they ask.

'Oh,' I say, 'nowhere special. Just hanging out with
a really famous person. They've gone now, but – they
hope to see me around!'

And that's the end of my daydream.

I've also imagined that I invite the famous person round so they can have a cup of tea.

But it doesn't quite work because Mum tends to get in a bit of a flap if anyone turns up unexpectedly. She worries if she hasn't hoovered.

Have you ever imagined having famous people over for tea – or maybe even for a full-on dinner party? Make a list of your top 10 favourite people you'd like to invite.

1. _____

2. _____

3. _____

4. _____

5. _____

6. _____

7. _____

8. _____

9. _____

10. _____

Our hero number 10, Martha, and her sister, Mary, invited the biggest celebrity of all time into their home – Jesus! He wasn't as well-known then as He is now, but crowds of people still followed Him all over the place.

Of course, it was an honour for Martha and Mary to have Jesus in their house. But He was also a friend of theirs, and of their brother, Lazarus, too.

Woah! If Jesus came to my house, that'd be it. I wouldn't do anything. Violin practice, homework… I wouldn't even watch TV! I'd just want to show Him round, chat to Him, listen to Him. And I'd want to take Him round to Sarah's so she could say hello too, *obviously*…

Mary was like that. The second Jesus stepped through the doorway, Mary dropped everything.

Whatever she was in the middle of – she just stopped.

Jesus sat down and Mary sat down too – at His feet to listen to Him.

SO… WHERE WAS MARTHA?

Even though Jesus was in her house, all Martha could think about was the washing and cleaning and cooking.

Everything Martha had to do was stressing her out. It was distracting her. It was getting in the way of her being able to spend time with Jesus.

There's always stuff in our heads. It's easy to get distracted when we sit down to read our Bible or talk to God. Or maybe we get distracted before we've even got to the 'sitting down with God' part!

Write down a few things here that might stop *you* spending time with God.

_____

_____

_____

_____

Like Martha, we need to decide what our priorities are. Below is a list of things that most of us do every day. Put them in order of how important you think they are (and they are *all* important!). There are no right or wrong answers – just have a think about what you would do first.

1 = I'd do this first   5 = I'd do this last

☐ Doing my homework

☐ Talking to God (praying)

☐ Helping around the house

☐ Reading my Bible

☐ Watching my favourite TV programmes

Martha may have got things a bit upside down, but Jesus didn't get cross. He didn't say, 'Well, if you haven't got time for me, I certainly haven't got time for you!'

He didn't storm out of Martha's house either, and never visit again.

In fact it was Martha who was a bit grumpy with Jesus: 'Don't you care that I've got all this work to do? Tell Mary to come and give me a hand!'

Jesus loved this family and He knew how much of a worrier Martha was.

Very kindly, Jesus told her to sort out her priorities. It was Mary who'd got things right. Mary was taking the time to stop and listen to His teaching. Jesus wanted Martha to do that too.

What could you do every day this week to help make God your top priority? Write it down, try it out and don't get distracted!

So, if Martha was a worrier who sometimes found it hard to make God her top priority, how could she be a hero for Him?

Well, **MARTHA'S BROTHER, LAZARUS, DIED.**

Even though Martha got distracted from God, she had amazing understanding about who Jesus was.

And her amazing understanding led her to have **HERO BELIEF** in Him. In other words, when it mattered most, Martha trusted Jesus.

Lazarus had been very ill. Martha and Mary sent for Jesus, but He didn't go to them straightaway. By the time He did get there, Lazarus had died.

But there was something Martha knew. Something she didn't doubt for an instant – if Jesus had been with Lazarus, he wouldn't have died.

She believed something else too, with her whole heart. Crack the code and write out the Bible verse to read what it was.

'▯ ⊃∀ ▯▽⊟▯∀◁∀ ⊕▷∧⊕ ⊞∀▯
∧◁∀ ⊕▷∀ ∆∀◁◁▷∧▷, ⊕▷∀
◁∀⊠ ∀▷ ⊙∀⊃'

_____

_____

_____

_____

Answer in John 11 v 27.

A	B	C	D	E	F	G	H	I	J	K	L	M
∧	▧	◉	⊃	▽	▷	⊙	▢	▯	◁	⊠	⊟	∆

N	O	P	Q	R	S	T	U	V	W	X	Y	Z
⊠	∀	▷	▷	◁	◁	⊕	⊡	◁	⊓	⊖	⊞	◁

In spite of all her worrying and times of not paying attention, Martha had got a lot of things about Jesus straight in her head.

So her brother had died and she was heartbroken. At the same time, because Lazarus was a friend of Jesus, the Son of God, she knew that one day he would be alive again with God in heaven.

The bit Martha didn't quite understand was that Jesus had the power to bring Lazarus back to life right there and then! And He went ahead and did it.

All Jesus had to say was… (Colour in the dotted shapes to find out!)

God made 100% sure that Martha's super-belief in her own personal hero was totally justified. And Jesus showed just how powerful God is. Jesus wasn't there to keep Martha's brother alive, but after Lazarus died, He was able to bring him back to life.

Martha knew Jesus' character so well because she'd spent time getting to know Him, and simply being His friend. But, guess what? All of us can enjoy that close friendship with God – it's not just for the heroes we read about in the Bible!

Sometimes it's easy to forget that we can ask Jesus *anything*. But we can – because He can do anything, and He loves us and wants what's best for us! We might not see people getting raised from the dead every day, but Jesus is always at work doing incredible things for and through us. Have you seen some answers to prayer? Why not write them down here to remind yourself what God has done for you?

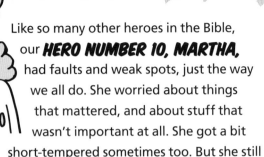

Like so many other heroes in the Bible, our **HERO NUMBER 10, MARTHA,** had faults and weak spots, just the way we all do. She worried about things that mattered, and about stuff that wasn't important at all. She got a bit short-tempered sometimes too. But she still understood who Jesus was. **SHE BELIEVED IN HIM, EVEN THROUGH A REALLY TOUGH TIME,** and knew that God's power was inside Him. And God didn't let her down.

The story of hero Martha teaches us:

- **To take time out to talk with and listen to God**

- **Not to get distracted from God by life stuff**

- **To know that we can give our worries to God**

- **To believe that God will always answer our prayers – in His time.**

Wow! What incredible heroes there are in the Bible. We've given you a peek into the lives of just 10 of them. Why not see if you can find out about a few more?

Here's a prayer for you to say today.

God, thank You for all Your Bible heroes. They were awesome! Not perfect people, but people who gave their lives to You and did their absolute best for You. God, I want to be a hero like that. Here is my life. Take me on an adventure with You today. Amen.

THERE ARE HEROES OUTSIDE THE BIBLE TOO!

God never stops – He's always at work in people! So here's a bit about two much more modern-day heroes.

JONI EARECKSON TADA

Do you know anyone with a disability? Or do you have a disability yourself? Some people are born disabled. For others, something happens to them. Maybe they get ill or have an accident.

Joni Eareckson Tada had a diving accident in 1967, when she was only 17 years old. Afterwards, she couldn't walk anymore or use her hands.

Joni spent two years learning how to live life a different way because of her disability. And she realised that God still had amazing plans for her.

Instead of hiding away, Joni set out to help other people with disabilities. She founded 'Joni and Friends', an organisation that teaches disabled people about God. It also teaches them how they can work for God in church and where they live, and shows churches what an important part every disabled person has to play.

Joni is a hero leader and worker for God. She must have wondered why something so terrible had happened to her, but God showed her that she could do the most incredible work.

And Joni didn't turn her back on Him. When God gave her a job to do, she said, 'Yes – I'm ready.'

CORRIE TEN BOOM

Corrie ten Boom was born into a Christian family in the Netherlands in 1892. The family served God by helping people in need.

During World War II, thousands of Jews were hunted down and killed. Some came to Corrie's house to ask for protection.

The family built a special place in their house where Jewish people could hide. This put her and her family in great danger, but that didn't stop them. They saved the lives of around 800 Jews.

One terrible day, the family were arrested for what they were doing. Corrie's father died in prison and she and her sister, Betsie, were sent to a concentration camp, where Betsie also died. But even as a prisoner, Corrie never stopped telling others about God.

After the war, Corrie showed even more hero strength. She not only helped other survivors of concentration camps, but also people who had worked there.

Corrie was able to forgive the people who had hurt her, because she knew that's what God wanted her to do.

You see, God's heroes are ordinary people, just like you and like me. But when we let God's power work inside us – that's when the hero stuff really starts to happen!

ANSWERS

Page 13

1. x
2. ✓
3. x
4. ✓
5. x
6. ✓
7. ✓
8. ✓

Page 16

1. Faithful
2. Loving
3. Patient
4. Kind
5. Hardworking
6. Unselfish

Page 19

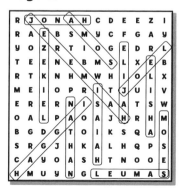

Page 23

1. ✓
2. ✓
3. x
4. ✓
5. x
6. ✓
7. x
8. x
9. ✓
10. ✓

Page 32

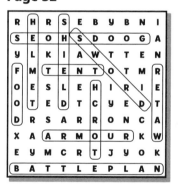

Page 45

Rahab put her own **life** in **danger** to **help** God's people. Rahab **trusted** God to look after her. Rahab **proved** her faith in God by **working** for Him.

Page 49

Proud – Humble
Happy – Sad
Selfish – Generous
Easy – Difficult
Fast – Slow
Quiet – Noisy
Boring – Exciting

Page 51

1. x
2. ✓
3. ✓
4. x

Page 57

Fisherman

Page 59

Say sorry to Jesus
Try hard not to do it again
Really mean it
Know that Jesus forgives you

Page 65

He kept on learning
He kept on trying
He stuck with Jesus

Page 68

1. x
2. ✓
3. x
4. x
5. ✓
6. ✓

Page 70

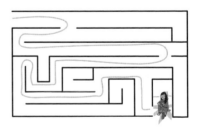

Page 81

Annoyed

Disgusted

Put out

Outraged

Insulted

Page 82

The woman knew she needed God's forgiveness, but Simon thought he was already perfect.

Page 84

1. B

2. B

3. A

4. C

Page 89

Unselfish

Kind

Brave

Caring

Honest

True

Loving

Loyal

Faithful

Page 94

1. False

2. True

3. True

4. False

5. True

6. False

Page 95

To check answers found in the Bible, you will need a Good News Bible. This version is available online.

TOPZ EVERY DAY

Topz is an exciting, day-by-day look at the Bible with the Topz Gang! Full of fun activities, cartoons, prayers and daily Bible readings – dive in and get to know God and His Word!

Available as an annual subscription or as single issues. Find out more at **www.cwr.org.uk/topzeveryday**

MORE TOPZ

There are four different series of *Topz* books for you to discover! Find out more at **www.cwr.org.uk/topzbooks**